LIBRARY
FUND-RAISING

LIBRARY MANAGEMENT SERIES

LIBRARY
FUND-RAISING:
VITAL MARGIN
FOR EXCELLENCE

edited by
Sul H. Lee

Dean, University Libraries
Professor of Bibliography
The University of Oklahoma

THE PIERIAN PRESS
1984

Library of Congress Catalog Card Number 84-60638
ISBN 0-87650-180-3

THE PIERIAN PRESS
P.O. Box 1808
Ann Arbor, MI. 48106

For Melissa

Contents

Introduction

Fund raising is an issue which draws increasing attention of academic and public library administrators. Even in publicly supported institutions the need for private funding to provide stability in budgets is critically important. To preserve the continuity necessary to build library collections and programs requires a commitment to fund these activities. Leaving the task of financial development to others may not be acceptable for survival of the library. The responsibility for extra outside curricular funding may come to rest with the library administrators.

The papers in this volume address theoretical and philosophical approaches to fund raising as well as some practical considerations. The logic and necessity of fund raising for libraries is a consistent theme throughout the volume. Yet, the stories of fund raising successes interweave with the more abstract reasonings for fund raising. One paper relates the establishment of a trust for a large public library. Two papers discuss fund raising philosophies in the libraries at large public universities. Another paper examines the important relationships with donors and successful programs in the library of a major private university. The final presentation is more of a kit to suggest proven fund raising strategies, to offer advice on organizing a fund raising program and to provide illustrations of letters, documents and other instruments used in a development campaign. Fund raising is normally very individual in approach and often situational. The political and economic climate of the beneficiary institution and its supporters as well as the institutional philosophy of development are paramount issues for the library management to consider. These papers do, however, offer a broad enough overview for introduction to fund raising. The papers were originally to be presented at a conference in October of 1983. Unfortunately, the conference could not be held. The value of the papers' contents did suggest the library community would benefit from their publication.

The authors of these papers represent organizations with a very fine record of achievement: Warren B. Kuhn is Dean of Library Services at Iowa State University; Robin Downes is Director of Libraries at the University of Houston; Pat Woodrum is Tulsa City-County's Library Director; Susan Getman Abernethy is Library Development Officer at Stanford University; and Albert Milano is General Manager of the Dallas Theater Center and President of The Milano Group, Inc.

Sul H. Lee
Norman, Oklahoma
January 30, 1984

EXCELLENCE IN THE EIGHTIES:
THE FUND-RAISING EXPERIENCE
AT IOWA STATE UNIVERSITY

Warren B. Kuhn

Fund-raising has always seemed to me to be not so much a strategy as a state of mind. When asked the inevitable question, "How can you stand going to people perpetually with your hand out?" the only answer can be: You go *out* with something *to give*, a *means* of preserving a memory, a *way* to repay the good things that have come your way in this life, an *opportunity* to remember others, someone, some place.

Lest this sound like moralizing, it should be added that such a state of mind must be honest. You must thoroughly believe in the quality and usefulness of what you are requesting; it must matter to you — personally, intensely. And while the quality of enthusiasm is essential to selling your success story — for that is what you are attempting to do, achieve the resources to make the project a success — plain enthusiasm is not enough. You need the ability to picture what will be and can be, not just the often sorry state of what it is you are trying to correct.

You must dream the impossible dream first, and then stimulate others to join with you in making that dream a reality. At Iowa State University our dream began with two men, both university presidents, both at Iowa State, both busy administrators faced with the demanding complexities of a modern, expanding institution. But beyond their daily chores, both had the ability to dream in very large fashion indeed, to look beyond the years to what should and could and would be accomplished. Both began with dreams and the ability to describe them to achieve the help they needed.

The first, the late President James Hilton, envisioned and lived to see a magnificent university center built entirely with funds contributed by alumni, friends, faculty, students and staff. The Iowa State Center now comprises a 2,700-seat auditorium pictured in *Time* magazine and capable of housing among other events an annual festival of world-famous symphonic orchestras, a 14,000-seat Coliseum, a little theater and a continuing education center, all heavily

1

used. Not a single penny of state funding was used in its construction.

The second, Iowa State's current President W. Robert Parks, is seeing the realization of his vision of a "new humanism" – a University eminently qualified for leadership in a technological age, successfully and sensitively joining its expertise in the sciences and humanities, equipped with greatly improved physical facilities and with Library resources now far better able to strengthen and sustain University excellence.

In earlier years the growth of the ISU Library had been much slower. By the mid-1960s there was a widening gap between the Library's condition and the growth of the University. Holdings were still solid and substantial, but the need for development had become a compelling concern. Thus in 1968, shortly after Parks became president, the University assumed as one of its primary goals the strengthening of the Library, and systematically began the underwriting of a large-scale acquisitions program.

In the decade that followed the Library experienced more than a doubling of its holdings, a larger faculty and staff and extensive internal improvements. But building space lagged inevitably behind this rapid growth. The situation had turned from overcrowding to crisis just at a time when the golden years of unviersity improvement were facing the tightening economic stringencies of the later seventies.

If there are principles to be listed in the lexicon of fund-raisers on university campuses, one most certainly is the absolute requirement for leadership at the very top. There rests the visibility whereby the need can be recognized. At Iowa State that leadership and that assistance have been superb. In the late spring of 1978 President Parks asked the Library to assemble its needs once again into a resource package for his use. There had been scores of documents, studies, annual reports, memoranda and letters that had been written, carefully buttressing the Library's case. These were refined, culled, abstracted. In addition, further research was done on such allied topics as the historical value of journals to university education and the changing face of librarianship; in all, a new distillation of the Library's own dream.

From this assemblage the President drew the most telling points in writing his annual convocation address for the year. That address given before the faculty and staff of the University and shared with alumni and friends across the country marked the kickoff of a new Library campaign. The address called attention to the central role of the Library within the University, the problems it was facing and the need for funds beyond those that could be expected from appropriations. It stressed again the importance of continuing Library

2

growth and development. "The quality and worth of every discipline," said Parks, "is tied into the quality and worth of the Library's holdings."

President Parks spoke dramatically of the Library's endless attempts to cope with its space problem: "Today the end of the road of coping and contriving has just about been reached. No more temporary solutions, however ingenious, can solve the growing space crisis the Library is experiencing. The Library has been living on borrowed time. The crisis is here. And it is up to the University to find a solution to this bedrock problem which will be adversely affecting this entire academic community. The only solution is, of course, the construction of a large, major addition to the Library. And this will be no easily achieved undertaking. For the dimensions of the Library's space and remodeling needs are so large-scale that any library building program will require heavy outlays of capital funds." Yet, Parks observed, neither the University nor the legislature could go it alone. As he phrased it, "Those qualities in structure and materials which are so generally the properties of the truly distinguished libraries must be gained by another road."

But, he felt, there was such a road at Iowa State University. He believed the Library could look forward to receiving substantial assistance from the University's alumni and friends who understood the importance to Iowa State of a quality library and were ready to take an active part in bringing about the Library's further development and improvement. He then announced that the Iowa State University Foundation "had taken on as a major goal the raising through voluntary contributions of $4,000,000, funds which are to be used to support and supplement the planning, equipping and construction of an addition to the Library." Part of that funding effort, $400,000, was immediately pledged by the members of the ISU Foundation's Board of Governors in order for the Library to begin architectural planning, the first such time in the history of the state that private funds were to be used for planning a major academic structure.

This, then, was the official beginning of what was termed the Library Fund drive. Its effort was directed and coordinated by the Development Office of Iowa State University and that office's diversified and extremely competent staff. In meetings between the Dean of Library Services and the Director of Development, an initial list of promotable areas was prepared, each with a suggested monetary goal, together with a campaign brochure and a series of donor levels for giving decided upon. Additional publicity, letters and visits in and out of state with alumni groups and individuals began to spread the word of the drive.

And here, as a second principle perhaps, of achieving a successful university fund-raising effort, we must underline the absolute importance of an imaginative, dedicated and respected development group on the campus. At Iowa State our truly excellent Development Office comprises both a very active and supportive Alumni Association and an equally imaginative and supportive Achievement Foundation. The latter combines an earlier Achievement Fund, which coordinated gift giving ranging from scholarship funds to annual drives, and an ISU Foundation which had concentrated on major gifts for "bricks and mortar." In recent years these joined together to provide a focused funding effort. Ongoing coordination of the Library Fund drive was in the hands of a member of the development staff, although constant and widespread support was provided by all Development Office members and University officers.

This variety of fund-raising directions and the ability of the Development Office to concentrate on distinct and separate funding goals while maintaining the widest range of individual contacts and visits has brought about spectacular results. Even as the coordinator of class gifts worked on individual class projects for the Library, those in charge of special projects were either visiting private corporations with the University story of which the Library was so much a part or accompanying the Dean of Library Services to small private foundations seeking grants for specialized equipment. The Development Office worked unceasingly in making personal and private contacts.

University development is a far more complex operation than the average person realizes: the responsibilities of and the time spent on maintaining liaison with alumni and donors are great. Communication between a university and its loyal alumni and friends is essential. Iowa State, as with all universities, not only maintains personal visits and alumni sponsored meetings across the country, but also encourages the return of alumni to the campus through alumni events, class reunions, homecoming and other celebrations. This closeness of Iowa State University and its alumni begins on campus with student alumni associations and a tradition of active participation of student fund-raising and sharing in the University's development.

Despite all this, it must be understood that a development office does not work in a vacuum. It must know your need, your requirements. Every person charged with fund-raising efforts on a university campus must be prepared to keep a constant flow of information going to the development office. For the Library at Iowa State, this means the most careful and continuing preparation of funding needs and especially the writing and communicating of them in a way that can be used by those soliciting gifts. These requests are short but full, telling in their description, and offer points of help on which specific contacts and requests can rest. This requires constant updating of lists of needs and gearing a specific need to a specific opportunity. When a contact is made by the development office, the fullest, concentrated attention by the library director is essential to outline needs in the most useful way possible. These range from a detailed letter answering a question from either on- or off-campus to preparing a major grant proposal in a few weeks' time. Each effort receives top priority in the library administrative office.

It should not be thought, however, that this activity at ISU has been of solely recent origin. Such a program from which the Library has benefited enormously has had many of its roots in the efforts of early alumni leaders who, working with the University, initiated scholarships and at their own expense traveled the nation bringing home to many the need for private support of the University. I sat with one of these wonderfully dedicated individuals recently as he recounted the visits he had made to his classmates more than thirty years ago, beginning in the 1950s. "One great problem we had to surmount," he recalled, "was the feeling that an individual had paid for his education once and for all when they had paid tuition and left the campus." The message he conveyed to them again and again instead was that the University was more than just a fond memory of autumn afternoons, football, friends and classrooms, that it was still a very personal part of each of them. They had a spiritual debt to repay. Such devoted personal efforts have culminated in much of the University's present private funding success. That alumnus is today not only an equally strong supporter of the Library but is providing the leadership in his class drive for a major memorial gift to us.

In 1982 Iowa State embarked on an even broader effort. On October 1 of that year the University inaugurated its largest campaign to date, that for "Excellence in the Eighties," a fund drive with a goal of $50,000,000 to be raised over five years. That same date happily coincided with a special evening tour of the Library's new addition, then fairly well along in construction; the tour consisted of a special group of alumni, University officials and friends, but more of that later. Thus University fund raising, building on its firm base of private support, was shifting much of the focus from its earlier desperate need for buildings to the heart of the University's academic requirements — the faculty, and the research and teaching tools they and their students needed, and emphasizing the provision of resources for the University to help such societal problems as those of the environment, energy and food supplies. As part of this positive new venture, the goal within the campaign for the Library became *at least* $1.1 million annually. This is the larger environment in which fund-raising for the Library at Iowa State University is currently being conducted.

5

The class gifts have been of major importance. The 50th Reunion alumni class each year has from the beginning of the Library fund drive responded magnificently. Their class effort is coordinated through a central gift committee which begins meeting several years in advance of the reunion date. Beginning with the Class of 1931, class members have chosen each year a special Library project for funding — their gift presentation being made at a special luncheon during the reunion celebration. The two most recent such gifts are examples of the success these alumni have had with this type of project. In 1982 the Class of 1932 presented the Library with a check for $34,000 to aid in the completion of a new photoduplication center and for a class memorial book fund. The latter part of the gift was provided by one class member alone.

This year the Class of 1933, following two years of careful preparation and leadership by a dedicated gift committee, made their gift of more than $102,000 to the Library for the purpose of further enhancing and furnishing a new Special Collections Reading Room, the largest such reunion class gift to date. And, the Class of 1934 has nearly reached their announced goal of $50,000 which will go toward final construction of a new Library Information Desk, exhibit cases and information kiosks for the expanded Library building.

At the heart of these efforts are the class leaders, the members of the gift committees who develop and maintain the class fund drives. Their members return frequently to campus to work with the Development Office, and their enthusiasm is contagious as we jointly develop plans and ideas to bring the drive to a rousing conclusion. While ostensibly retired, the gift committee members are, nevertheless, very busy people, yet they manage to return regularly for campus meetings. The value of these visits cannot be understated. One hard-working committee member told me after a special tour in which he had had for the first time a chance to see what the class was funding, "If we had all seen what was being done in the Library, I'm sure we would have done even more." Shortly thereafter, he held a committee picnic at his home at which he sought and received additional contributions to raise his class total even higher. And this occurred on the very eve of the class reunion!

Important, too, is the opportunity for these grant people to see and share in the finished product. Each year during reunions we provide special tours of the Library for not only the reunion gift class but all others as well. I have also begun to provide a single page outline for reunion classes which describes in hopefully vivid language what the gift will do for use by the gift committee in their solicitation.

Class gifts by students still on campus also contribute to the fund

6

campaign. Each senior class at Iowa State appoints a class gift committee early in the senior year. These students marshall ideas, one of which is chosen by class vote for their primary funding effort. Students pledge contributions for the first five years after graduation, the funds accumulating in the Development Office interest-bearing accounts. These funds can be released for ongoing work on the chosen project or held until the end of the pledge period when the total amount is released. We tend to leave as much of these and other funds in investment accounts as are not immediately needed. In some instances these funds have replenished themselves so well as to serve almost as interim endowments in themselves.

The Library has been fortunate in being the recipient of senior class gifts for the initiation of a collection of music and sound recordings for a new Library media center, for support of media stereophonic listening rooms, and for other library areas such as group studies. In 1978, long before the new addition became an active construction project, the Library mapped out the recording collection idea for the class of that year which responded enthusiastically. Today the Library is using $4,000 of the accumulated funds to begin the ordering of the first recordings and tapes which will form the Class of 1978 Music and Spoken Word Collection at Iowa State.

Another student-sponsored effort may well be unique at Iowa State. Each year the Greek Societies on campus begin making plans for an event-packed Greek Week festival held in the spring. A crowning part of the effort is conducting special fund-raising for a Greek service project. A coordinating committee enlists the aid of more than three hundred student volunteers from all sororities and fraternities who conduct a two- or three-week evening "callathon," telephoning Greek alumni across the country. Local merchants donate a special prize for the Greek house achieving the greatest dollar total. In addition, special mailings are made both to alert alumni to the effort being made and later to follow up on those who were not at home when called. Our Development Office provides facilities, phones and coordination of the massive record-keeping this entails.

Each year I have been fortunate to meet with the coordinators of these projects, each year outlining a new suggested area for their consideration. Other campus areas, of course, are also being considered. One does not work in a vacuum on campus, nor without competition. Ideas must be presented with care and imagination if they are to be accepted and pursued successfully.

In 1980 the ISU Greek Societies provided support for a new book reading room in the Library; in 1981 the project centered on a reading room for the visually impaired; in 1982 on the remodeling of a Grant Wood Heritage area; and in 1983 the project was restoration of a new student study lounge in which part of the Library's leisure reading collection will be located. In each circumstance I prepared a profile of the project and its importance which was used in the mailings of the Greeks. To see these young people in action, conveying their enthusiasm to alumni across the country and urging support for a Library project, is the greatest stimulus any fund raiser can desire. We are deeply grateful to these students not only for the success they achieve but also for the remarkable efforts they make.

The focus of such individualized drives, of course, is on what is chosen. While the coordinating committees of all of these groups first meet with Development Office staff, it is left up to the dean, director or other involved individuals to provide every opportunity for ideas and needs to be discussed and examined. Obviously it is important to portray the need convincingly. Where a building is involved, if far enough along in construction, its physical presence can be a great help. In many cases, and indeed most, however, one must paint a picture verbally in the strongest possible way and stress its value to the University and the educational process. In the case of students still on campus, they know of many of the needs personally. They have lived with the lacks, the gaps and the problems, and it is to their great credit that they take time from their hectic schedules to work toward solving these problems which in almost every instance can only benefit later generations of students and not themselves. It is a selfless, wonderful spirit they display.

Not all our fund-raising is a collective effort, naturally. Many superb gifts come through individuals who while dedicated to the University are made aware of needs through campaigns such as those just described. Several gifts have added immeasurably to our rare book collections. Others have initiated family-sponsored book funds or funds provided by groups of friends honoring a chosen individual. In at least one instance the strength of one magnificent individual's belief in the Library's need permitted him, a successful and innovative engineer and industrialist, to assist decisively in concentrating alumni action on the Library's space problems and culminated in his becoming a devoted, driving force toward a remarkable class gift. All of these individual acts and those of the classes and the Greek Societies create exceptional models for emulation; they establish perfect examples of what *can be done*. Before one gets carried away with the success of a funding campaign, however, it must be realized that long before it and you arrived, the spirit and quality of the institution had been effectively and quietly providing an appropriate reason for funding. And that many individuals had been laboring and giving equally quietly of themselves and their funds.

The Library's largest gift and bequest to date, eventually to total more than one-half million dollars, was made by a quiet and wonderful couple who wanted to recognize what the University had meant to them and who selected the Library as representing the heart of the institution. Their gift was made years before the formal campaign. Similarly, other alumni had established scholarship funds quietly and without fanfare decades before the emergence of funding campaigns. These same individuals continue in that same selfless vein to support the University and the Library. Happily, the new campaign permits ongoing and renewed recognition of such gifts.

Recognition can take many forms. In a building the most obvious is through naming the reading room, the study lounge or the faculty study. Handsome and unique plaques are ideal vehicles for this purpose. However, the imagination should not be fettered to thoughts of only enclosed spaces. The ISU Class of 1934 will be recognized for its gift of a granite and oak information desk, two internally-lit exhibit cases and a main floor information kiosk with specially-designed changeable graphics, all with polished black granite bases. Other pending gift ideas cover open reading alcoves overlooking our library addition's new atrium. We even hope to attract donors to name a lovely internal bridge across the atrium connecting our old and newer buildings. Gift funds have supported the acquisition of sculpture for the Library which will bear a plaque recognizing the donor. We have even memorialized a computer terminal!

The single most important form of recognition, and the one with the greatest immediacy, of course, is the not so simple letter of thanks. I personally believe these are of the utmost importance, and I attempt to spend a good deal of time on each, making them both personal and focused upon the area of the gift. Too often letters of gift acknowledgment are far too short and automatic; the result is depressingly lifeless. They convey nothing of the warmth of you as the writer nor of your sense of appreciation; the institutional spirit you are underscoring is also lacking. You cannot say thank you often enough to the giver; honest repetition of your gratitude should shine — SHINE — through the entire letter. It is a perfect medium for you to show your personal interest in the donor and the gift.

If you are committed to your project and would succeed in fundraising, you must become a prolific correspondent, bringing each donor up-to-date on where plans are going, what is happening in your Library and how the donor is contributing to its success. My administrative assistant and I keep a shelf of letter copies alphabetically and chronologically arranged in looseleaf notebooks. While voluminous, they are far easier to consult than files for this purpose, concentrating your Library's donors and information about them and their support in one location. The matter of recognition is important in fund-raising, of course, but it is far from the sole reason for giving. People give to a campaign such as Iowa State's because they believe in an institution and its principles. They deserve every bit of recognition and appreciation; yet in the final analysis their loyalty to the institution and their faith in it and you are the unmatchable factors.

All this said, it is still imperative that the gift idea be made tangible to those whose lives are normally spent far from the everyday demands of university programs. The idea of the gift in its nascent stages to deserve support must be explained in a way that can be easily understood. In many cases the end product – a finished building, a significant collection, a dramatically-furnished study area or a computer system – is usually a vague concept when a drive begins and one that changes even while it is underway. Visualizing the end result for donors can be far from simple. One method of helping others visualize the dream for which support is sought is by a brochure. Iowa State began with simple ones of single color, then inaugurated its "Excellence" campaign with a stunning one with color photography. The Library is now planning one of similar dimension focusing on its needs. We intend to make it attractive but unusual.

Brochures need not be costly to be effective. One very reasonably-priced brochure prepared for an alumni class campaign of ours consisted of an unpretentious 5 by 8-inch leaflet bearing on its cover a black-and-white photograph of an 1854 lithograph of American Indians. Not only was the original lithography beautifully done and well worth using, but the picture was also one from a three-volume set of portraits that once hung in the Indian gallery of the U.S. War Department, the originals of which were destroyed by fire in 1865. ISU owns the set. The recounting of this story in the brochure added to the tone of rarity and preservation we were attempting to convey. The brochure, designed for a mailing for the 50th Anniversary Gift of the ISU Class of 1933, described the Library's Special Collections Reading Room as the subject of the proposed gift and included sample names of important persons whose manuscripts and papers are held by Special Collections. A small photograph of a Dickens' first edition was also included as a further sample of the rare works in our collection. The rear page listed the members of the class gift committee. The photographs were taken by the Dean, saving the further cost of commercial photography, and the entire brochure printed by a local card shop at very low rates. I remember vividly standing precariously on a library table in my stocking feet, focusing with a macro Nikon lens on the rarities spread out on the table on which I was standing. The brochure was carefully written but quickly produced.

Another piece done for our campaign planners was a handbook developed as a guide for members of the alumni office staff and others who, perhaps not as familiar with the Library plans as Library staff, needed something ready at hand when talking with donors either by phone or in person. Entitled, "Building Toward the Year 2000," the handbook contained a list of potential areas for gifts, grants and bequests. Since our building remodeling was to be in two phases, these phases were also described in a foreword. Both the new library addition and the renovation of the present building had all possible gift areas listed by floor with the dollar level of gift suggested. As the campaign proceeded, donors, date of the gift or pledge and the amount given were also included for internal purposes. A special section was added covering nonbuilding items in the campaign such as book endowments and funds for automation. Each building area was numbered, the number referring to pages in the handbook where the area or room was succinctly described. At the rear of the handbook floor diagrams were included with these same locations bearing the same numbers for each reference.

The resulting package thus gave each staffer, student or alumni leader a simple reference guide to some of the Library's major needs, provided a brief and descriptive section about the gift to paint the picture for any possible donor, and later included color photographs taken as the building progressed. It was felt to be a handy and useful guide as the campaign got underway.

People want to be associated with success. This is just as important for libraries and their fund-raising campaigns as it is for football teams. Thus visible results of gift giving and the environment they can create are also important. For this reason tours at Iowa State of the new addition have formed a major part of our initial fund-raising effort. Even after the opening of the partially remodeled building, we have maintained these special tours and exhibits to continue that fine sense of excitement so necessary to the impetus of any campaign. Other libraries long in this business do this equally well with remarkable grace, bonhomie and success.

One special event of this nature at Iowa State was the visit by a large and very special group of alumni and friends to our partially finished new library addition in the fall of 1982. The event was part of the annual fall meeting of the Order of the Knoll, Iowa State University's most prestigious group of friends. Begun in 1968, this group which initially met in the President's home now must meet in the University's large Coliseum, for the group has grown to nearly 1,500 persons! The 1982 meeting centered on a very large assembly of special faculty exhibits of research, work in progress, scientific displays and similar exciting things to see on the floor of our Coliseum, preceded by the special visit and tour of the library addition. Two major campaign gifts, done by personal check, were made on that very evening!

As part of the Library tour, the contractor, despite uncooperative rainy fall weather, managed to pour the final main entry sidewalks in what was remarkably hair-breadth timing, and the special visitors brought by buses from the Coliseum were able to enter the new front doors of the Library with the splendid view of the beautiful new building before them. Staff greeted them, separated them into small groups for more personalized tours, and presented each with a special brochure listing pertinent facts about the building, highlights of interest on each floor and the building's many unique and innovative features. Remodeling ideas occupied the final page of this brochure with a low-keyed plea for further funding. The cover bore a photograph of the new addition's limestone facade. Since that special tour, the brochure has been updated and used continuously for a host of other visiting groups. It has proven to be a valuable item for building information and a fine take-away piece for interested persons.

Another very visible avenue of gift giving lies, of course, with the collections and their enduring nature. Every librarian can recount innumerable successes in this area, particularly with rare works and manuscripts. Iowa State has been very fortunate in the interest of alumni who very rightly see such gift giving for acquisitions as fundamental to the University's purpose.

The Library's millionth volume, Leonardo da Vinci's *Trattato della Pittura*, his treatise on painting, was made possible by a book fund subscribed to by the friends of a remarkable and incredibly talented alumnus, the founder of a major industrial concern in Iowa and patron of the arts nationwide. This fund, devoted in the broadest sense to art and the humanities, has permitted continuing purchases in these subjects in addition to the millionth volume. In developing a bookplate for these volumes, an oil portrait of the honoree was re-sketched permitting a striking and unusual plate. In addition, we reproduced the portrait in smaller size together with a brief biography of the person on a distinctive two-colored bookmark. Each work purchased by the fund holds one of the bookmarks, and our earnest hope is that they be taken by our readers as constant reminders of how a book fund can serve to honor and recognize as well as to support library development.

In another unique instance a loyal and wonderful alumni friend had heard of the limited publishing venture that recently reproduced the Michelangelo Frescoes from the Vatican. A world-traveled engineer and steadfast supporter of the University and the Library, he immediately underwrote the cost of the book, still unpublished, of which only three hundred copies were to be available in the United States. Iowa State is now one of approximately three dozen libraries who hold the Frescoes in this format.

My final comments lie with our attempt to provide a packaged video program for use statewide and nationally with alumni and other friends. From the beginning of the addition's construction, I had been taking color photographs of building progress from excavation through column pouring, glazing and finishing. My thought was to prepare a slide and audio presentation. However the bulkiness of slides, their tendency toward possible loss or damage and the increasing use of educational television on our campus tempted me to try an experiment. We are fortunate to have an excellent media resources group at Iowa State, and after writing the script and choosing some of the music, I began work with a young graduate student employee of the campus media resources organization who by the use of video techniques, zoom-cameras and other techniques was able to turn the several years of accumulated photography into a single, compact ¾-inch video tape. Admittedly, I am told, the initial idea of a dean wanting his own undoubtedly awkward snapshots turned into something remotely usable was greeted by queasiness and furrowed brows among our media professionals. The silk purse they produced however, is a credit to what a media specialist can do.

The tape was produced in about two week's time, and we had our share of gray hairs in winnowing out the hundreds of slides, giving them some continuity and trying, at times not too successfully, to hide the fact that the finished building was still in the hands of the workmen. I'm afraid the glass clamps still show, the windows are obviously dusty and there is a definite speckling of plywood panels where glass had been removed or was broken. The maiden showing of the tape was for a meeting of the Iowa State Board of Regents and was quite successful. Since that time, the program has continued to be well received and is proving ideal for alumni meetings across the country.

The most important point I want to make about the tape is the minimal cost of its production, the ease with which we can reproduce it for both safety and for duplicate showings, and the appeal that local photography, music and sound can have even for the casual viewer. It was fun to do and an experiment we intend to repeat in some fashion.

It has been discussed from several angles, but it all adds up to fund-raising being satisfying and immensely rewarding. On top of that, one works with fine and responsive people, and whether they can help support the cause or not, they are people you instinctively want to treat royally. Whether students, alumni, faculty or friends, they are people to whom help is not just a four letter word. Can you ask for anything better than that?

GIFTS, GRANTS, AND GRANTORS:
GARNERING THE LIBRARY'S SHARE

Susan Getman Abernethy

While traveling in the East a few months ago, I stopped in Lexington, Massachusetts to visit a friend, saw the monument to the Minuteman on Lexington green, and visited an art gallery, the Gallery on the Green. In the gallery I found a work of art whose title seemed the perfect metaphor for Lexington and its role in American history as well as for the following remarks on fund-raising for academic libraries. The work of art was titled "Oh let our dreams soar high and free!"[1] I doubt the English artist realized in advance the subtle irony of having her work with that title for sale in an American art gallery a stone's throw from the site of the first battle of the American revolution – Oh let our dreams soar high and free. However, the phrase about daring to dream is an apt guideline for what must be done in the realm of development for research libraries.

To me the term "development" is preferred to "fund-raising." Development is an especially accurate and comprehensive term for our efforts to build our library collections, facilities, and service capacity through gifts and grants. In libraries we want to encourage gifts of appropriate materials (and sometimes equipment) as well as gifts of dollars. So we do more than fund-raising. I feel that library gift-raising and grant procurement are best thought of as library development.

One of the virtues of thinking in terms of development and not merely money is in making a claim on the time and creativity of many librarians in addition to the library director and the library development officer. For example, special collections librarians can be helped to see that gifts of desired materials do not often come over the transom but are more likely to result from sustained and focused contact with collectors and other holders of desired materials. It is the responsibility of the relevant library staff to help the library development officer identify potential donors of materials and to help create a climate of awareness among collectors that the library is interested in their materials and is a worthy repository for these gifts — if you can honestly say that you are proud of your conditions for environmental monitoring, security, bibliographic access, and other aspects of stewardship of rare materials. (If you are not proud of these conditions and want to improve them, you might find a collector who will make a monetary gift to enable you to achieve improved quarters.) What the library development officer can do is offer guidance on how to foster mutually satisfying relationships with prospective donors of collections, how to bring people closer to the university and to the library, and how to make the actual request for the gift if the collector seems slow in self-soliciting. But the continuing contact with the prospective donor is most effectively sustained by the librarians, not by the library development officer, in most cases. Development done well is development done collaboratively.

You will notice that I assume that each university has a library development officer, either someone on the office of development staff assigned part-time to the library or, as at Stanford, a full-time library development officer who coordinates work with the main office of development. I also assume substantial involvement by the library director because donors often want to talk with or hear from no one other than the person at the top. Primary responsibility for development cannot be delegated further down the chai.

In the ensuing examples and reflections, I shall use Stanford University and my five-plus years as library development officer there as the experience base. Since each university is different in some important ways from other universities, I do not intend for my views to be prescriptive of what others should do. I simply offer examples, not intending for you to see them necessarily as exemplary. And I am indulging in examples rather than presenting a more general outline of library development because there are excellent printed sources for theory about library development. There are full citations for some sources at the end of the paper but, in brief, I would point particularly to an ALA publication, *Funding Alternatives for Libraries*,[2] that emanated from a workshop on fundraising for libraries held almost eight years ago at Pratt. Some of the papers in *Funding Alternatives for Libraries* are more suited to public library development than to research library development (and particularly research libraries in institutional settings, where access policies are controlling), and some of the specifics are dated. But the majority of the book provides a good general base and is well worth reading. Since the volume lacks an index, I will recommend two chapters, the short one on "Operating within a Parent Institution" by the editors of the book, Breivik and Gibson, and the longer chapter on "Fund Raising for University Libraries" by Andrew J. Eaton.

Eaton's paper was actually written earlier and appeared in *College & Research Libraries* in 1971.[3] Eaton's advice seems to be basically sound. Since he was library director at Washington University and wrote the paper on a grant from the Council on Library Resources, perhaps readers who are library directors will particularly appreciate his insights. Other chapters in this book contain some how-to information that is useful. Any book and any article such as this will run the risk of seeming to state the obvious. I want to emphasize that each library in its own institutional setting, within that institution's ground rules, will decide for itself what its needs are that might be met by a development plan and which ones cannot be met through gifts, Each library will go through the long consultative process of determining its priorities. Each library will decide within its own budget and according to its own style how to articulate its needs — in brochures, reports, and meetings with advisory groups and prospective donors.

Gifts

First let me sketch a picture of the situation at Stanford University. Recently Stanford celebrated the acquisition of its five millionth book and the tenth anniversary of the library friends group, The Associates of the Stanford University Libraries. The Associates group has over 700 memberships, mostly in California and predominantely in the San Francisco Bay area where Stanford is located. The group can be characterized as dream-soaring and vigorous, offering about ten programs a year on Sunday afternoons followed by receptions in the Lurie Rotunda, the Special Collections exhibit area. This is in the Cecil H. Green Library which houses the main humanities and social science research collections as well as the Jonsson Library of Government Documents, the University Archives, and the technical processing and administrative areas for the library system. Since the Associates are organized to support the whole library system and not focus exclusively on special collections, they usually hold at least one meeting a year in a branch or other library outside Green Library, and they make a gift of materials worth up to $200 to the library they visit; the materials are chosen by the librarian of that branch.

Larger gifts are made by the Associates group on landmark occasions, such as a manuscript of Ovid's *Metamorphoses* on the occasion of the dedication of the new wing of Green Library three years ago; a manuscript collection of statutes of the city of Marseilles when the renovated department of Special Collections was dedicated two years ago; and, with help from others, the five millionth book. Over the ten years of its life, and excluding the five millionth book, the

Associates as a group have made gifts worth $60,000. This might seem like a disappointingly low figure, an average of $6,000 a year. But I believe that this will rise as the group gains experience with its recently-established pattern of biennial fund-raising events such as book fairs and book auctions.

More fundamentally, the Stanford library administration views the Associates' value not so much in group terms as in individual terms. Associates members as individuals have made desirable gifts of materials from their own collections, and although it is rarely possible to document with any certainty a causal relationship in the world of development, my strong hunch is that many, if not most, of these gifts would not have come to Stanford if the individuals had not become involved with librarians through attending enjoyable and interesting trips, programs, and seminars sponsored by the group, if they had not read interesting book- and library-related articles in the excellent volunteer-produced semi-annual publication *Imprint*, had not rubbed shoulders with other collectors making gifts of materials to Stanford, had not seen favorable publicity about gifts in the *Annual Report of the Stanford University Libraries* (sent to all Associates members), and had not felt part of a successful enterprise. Besides making gifts of materials from their own collections or serving as information sources to the librarians about other collections that might be available as gifts, a few members of the Associates have made gifts of endowed book funds in their own names, have served as information sources for the library development officer, and as volunteers in soliciting others for book funds. They have also served as Stanford Library advocates with foundations with whom they have influence. Individuals also volunteer their time to keep the Associates going, to run the programs and staff the fundraising benefits and, within the Library, to conduct book sales in Gifts and Exchanges, participate in the Brittle Books Program in the Conservation Office, check in materials in the Serials Department, select appropriate volumes to carry Memorial and Celebration Fund bookplates from among the accepted materials on the approval shelves, and inventory and encapsulate maps in the Department of Special Collections. In all these instances of volunteer work within the Library, the Associates members have the satisfaction of performing a worthwhile task, interacting with Library staff, and feeling more involved with Stanford.

Although the Associates as a group might not seem cost-beneficial from some library administrators' standpoints, the Stanford University Libraries' administration views the effectiveness of the Stanford Library Associates as being mostly what individual members can do for the Library over the long run. An excellent overview of "Friends Groups and Academic Libraries" was written by Paul

Mosher as part of an Allerton Park Institute four years ago and is available in the proceedings, *Organizing the Library's Support: Donors, Volunteers, Friends.*[4]

I mentioned the long run. Development done well is not only done collaboratively but patiently. Sometimes it is many years between the beginning of a relationship between an individual and the library and any fruit from the relationship in the form of a lifetime gift of a significant collection, a major gift of funds or a bequest of a collection or funds. An aside at this point would be to caution libraries not to lose heart if the lifetime gift or bequest of a library friend is designated for a non-library purpose within the university. It is understood at Stanford that the library offers an excellent donor-relations opportunity for the University to maintain and foster contact with individuals. It is possible that someone's main interest would be a named professorship in the School of Engineering, and he would make a gift for that purpose; but his avocational delight in book collecting makes him take pleasure in the company of like-minded people at Library Associates meetings or library-sponsored seminars. And it is also possible that without the library relationship the donor would have no meaningful relationship with Stanford and therefore would not be inclined to make the gift of the professorship. Thus the library must adopt and maintain an institutional viewpoint about its activities, not a narrow, library-focused one. This is one of several reasons for my favoring the personnel arrangement at Stanford where the library development officer's salary is shared by the library and the office of development. Such a shared arrangement ensures that both units of the University take responsibility, makes the staff member feel part of both units, and helps acknowledge the broader utility of the library's development activities.

I should point out that Stanford was founded just under one hundred years ago. That may sound like antiquity to some libraries; for example, the San Diego campus of the University of California was opened in La Jolla within the last twenty years. But compared with our peer institutions in the East, Stanford is relatively young. Another aspect of our profile is that Stanford has traditionally emphasized the sciences and engineering. Many Stanford alumni have excelled in the technical fields and gone on to found successful high-tech companies in the area near Stanford (the so-called "Silicon Valley") and elsewhere. The combination of being "young" and known more for the scientific and technical fields than for the humanities and social sciences is a combination of factors with significant implications for the library. In the past twenty years Stanford has refined a collection development policy statement, performed collection evaluations, and accelerated retrospective purchasing to improve the humanities collections. That situation made the library an enthusiastic participant in the University's proposal for a Challenge Grant from the National Endowment for the Humanities in 1977. A Challenge Grant was awarded in 1978 and, with the advantage of the grace year, completed successfully in 1982.

I shall go into some detail about the NEH Challenge Grant because it was a very constructive experience for library development at Stanford. The library part of the institutional goal was $900,000 in three years. NEH matched on a one-third basis, i.e., NEH gave Stanford $1 for every $3 raised. Because the University transferred part of another unit's goal to the library toward the end, and we met it, the library raised $954,621; NEH gave the library $318,207. The combined new resources earmarked for the humanities in the library at Stanford amounted to $1,272,828. The Library raised over $950,000, but no all of that was money; more than a third of it came in the form of the appraised value of gifts-in-kind that met the NEH criteria of being in the humanities and from donors who had not given to Stanford before. It is evident why I am a believer in encouraging gifts of significant collections: in this case they not only added to Stanford's intellectual resources but also added to the library's financial resources in the humanities by drawing matching funds from NEH. A collection appraised at $100,000 would earn for the library $33,333 in funds from NEH. The matching funds from gifts-in-kind were used to establish new endowed book funds in the name of the donor of the collection, thus giving the donor the pleasure of a "double gift" and the benefit of a long-term relationship with the library because of the donor-relations and gift recognition activities which will be described later.

In accordance with the terms of the Challenge Grant, the funds raised and the NEH funds must be spent in acquisitions for the humanities — either on an expendable basis or through endowed income. This was precisely what the library was "dreaming" of doing or it would not have gone to the trouble of competing for the Challenge Grant and the trouble of completing it. The NEH grant was trouble. The rules for donor eligibility were complicated and difficult to convey to the volunteer group we assembled to help with the task. The record-keeping within the University was painstaking and had to be so in order to document gifts, matching funds, account numbers, and the proper transfer of funds from the NEH holding account to the individual endowed or expendable accounts. NEH required that donors sign a standard letter of transmittal. The experience was all much more bureaucratic, for lack of a more precise term, than development people are comfortable about putting volunteers and donors through.

Despite the frustrating elements of the NEH Challenge Grant, I for one am ready to proclaim the benefits of such a program.

Stanford gained twenty-four new endowed book funds in the humanities, and I wonder if we could have sustained such a push for new funds without the incentive of a matching grant and without the accompanying threat of forfeiture of matching funds if each year's goal was not met. (The Challenge Grant had interim goals in twelve-month periods, and if the interim goal were unmet, one would have to give up the opportunity of earning that year's unmatched dollars.) Another benefit of the Challenge Grant was the loyalty to the library of the nine committee members who stayed the course under a dedicated volunteer chairman for three and a half years. We hope to count on that loyalty in the coming years and will undoubtedly ask some of these same volunteers to help with new tasks. In addition to the library development officer, the library staff member of the committee was Paul Mosher, whose position as Associate Director for Collection Development gave him an overview of collection needs. Two eminent faculty members from humanities departments were active members of the committee. They in turn enlisted occasional assistance from eight other faculty members from the humanities, chosen to represent different departments and for their personal enthusiasm and ability to articulate the necessity of excellent library collections. Another benefit of the Challenge Grant effort was the manifest willingness of many faculty to help with library development activities. I acknolwedge there is an element of faculty self-interest in this enterprise as far as faculty in the humanistic fields are concerned; the less library-dependent faculty in the scientific and technical fields might not be as avid as the humanists in fund-raising and collection development for libraries. The fact remains, however, many faculty members gave a good deal of time, thought, and energy to help us achieve the NEH goal. We hope this faculty friendship for the library grows even stronger over the years.

Still another benefit of the NEH Challenge Grant was greater understanding of development by the library staff as a whole and particularly by the librarians whose work intersects with the humanities. Just as it was in the faculty's interests to help identify prospective donors, help plan strategies for solicitation, and speak at seminars to which we invited prospective donors, so too was it in the librarians' interest to provide information for proposals, think in financial terms, meet with prospective donors, and display collegial enthusaism when gifts came in and periodic progress reports were made. A certain solidarity among the staff is a pleasant by-product of a campaign like the NEH Challenge Grant.

Having mentioned the helpfulness of volunteers during the NEH Challenge Grant, I want to recognize an on-going group of volunteer advisors, the Visiting Committee to the Stanford University Libraries. The Committee has some thirty members, including two Trustees, serving three-year terms in rotation. It meets once a year and submits its report to the president of the University. The Visiting Committee has five subcommittees, including one on Resources, which is staffed by the library development officer. The Resources subcommittee serves as a very helpful sounding board for ideas, a source of information about potential gifts, and a source of interested volunteers who are willing to be called on for advice, advocacy or bringing a prospective donor closer to the University. The subcommittee reviews the list of gift needs in the library and offers comments on the likely degree of success of achieving the desired objectives; most members of the committee are experienced development volunteers.

This section on gifts will conclude with a few other facts about library development at Stanford. Memorial gifts are directed to the library unless the donor makes a specific request to the contrary, such as financial aid. The Memorial Fund and the Celebration Fund — for gifts in tribute of living individuals or in honor of occasions such as anniversaries or retirements — are both in the library series of accounts. On a bookplate the library lists the name of the donor and the name of the person in whose memory or honor the gift is made. We suggest and usually receive a minimum gift of $25 and often much more for these gifts. Memorial Fund income is in the neighborhood of $30,000 a year.

Stanford's minimum gift requirement for a named endowed fund for acquisitions or conservation is $10,000. For this we commission a unique bookplate that reflects the donor's interests and taste, from the colorful to the subdued. I am in favor of this relatively low figure as the endowment requirement because it attracts 1) donors who cannot afford more initially but often add to their fund if the library does a good job of reporting to them and 2) donors who wish to test the waters of the library and, once satisfied, add generously to the fund that they have established.

Gifts to the library in the range of $100 to $1,000 that are not specifically restricted are often directed by the library administration to conservation. This is done in the knowledge that the gift will be used to provide preservation treatment for a work or works whose titles can be sent by letter to the donor in the hope that he or she will become interested in library conservation. Someone interested is of course someone more likely to make additional gifts. A typewritten book label with the name of the donor and the year of the gift is placed in works whose preservation was made possible by gift funds. This is a long-term, low-key method of attempting to set a philanthropic example for readers who use materials restored through gift funds.

Moving on to the second word in the title of this paper, "Gifts, Grants, and Grantors," helpful information about the grant-seeking process with respect to foundations, corporate foundations, and federal agencies is available in Richard W. Boss's book, *Grant Money and How to Get It; A Handbook for Librarians.* [5] This is admittedly an elementary book, and it is written more for public libraries than for those in institutional settings with development offices staffed by professionals, but it offers a useful review of points to keep in mind and lists of foundations known to be sympathetic to libraries. The problem with such lists is that they go out of date, often do not reveal some important constraints, and are incomplete. Your office of development or sponsored projects office will be able to provide a good deal of information about grant request preparation and placement, application deadlines, board meeting cycles, and known interests for the larger foundations or ones with which your university already has contact. For the smaller or lesser-known foundations or ones that want to maintain a low profile, information from and advocacy by Associates members and other friends of the library can make the difference.

I believe it is important for librarians, not the library development officer, to draft grant proposals. The library development officer may edit the work for marketability, but the ideas, facts, and persuasive argument for the project must come from the library staff. That being the case, and grant proposals tending to be time-consuming to write, we have handled only a few small grants — in the range of $10,000 to $50,000 — and only a few large ones. In addition to the previously-mentioned NEH Challenge Grant, Stanford has been fortunate to receive generous support from the grant program administered by the Higher Education Act, Title II-C; a joint grant from the Sloan and Mellon Foundations shared by the University and the University of California at Berkeley to establish a cooperative program with several components; and a grant from the Mellon Foundation to establish a conservative administration internship program that will bring to Stanford one intern per year for the next three years. Mellon has given a similar conservation internship grant to a handful of other libraries. Recently Stanford was awarded a grant by the Council on Library Resources to conduct a study of database searching. We have submitted a proposal to NEH for help with an important archival processing project that will relate to a similar project funded by NEH last spring.

The other point that I wish to make about grants, in addition to the view that the responsibility for conceptualizing and writing the proposals should rest with the library staff whose immediate work will benefit from the grant, is a point about the political setting in which the library exists. This differs among institutions, of course, and particularly between independent and public institutions and between those operating in a centralized fashion and those which do not. However, we all operate in a political setting. At Stanford the Provost's Office approves projects for the gift opportunity list throughout the University and, in consultation with the foundations and corporations staff in the office of development, sets the priorities for what areas of the University may submit a gift or grant request to which foundations and when. The library may have a very worthy project that has received the provost's approval as a gift opportunity, but if the project is an automated circulation system, it is not likely to be approved for submission to a major foundation that *is* likely to be captivated by the idea of funding some breakthrough medical research, for example. Or, if submission of the request is approved but the office of development foundations staff decides to submit the library proposal along with a medical proposal, it is not unusual for that foundation to select the medical project over the library one. It is a fact that while many of a research library's needs are significant, they are simply not exciting, which is a dilemma for libraries trying to get the attention of their development offices or of foundation program officers or boards. This is partly what is meant by"garnering the library's share." Libraries must acknowledge, I believe, that endowed book funds are fairly saleable to individual donors, library facilities are a little harder for which to obtain gifts or grants, and library service improvements such as retrospective cataloging conversion and large-scale automation are especially difficult — mostly because they are seen as maintenance projects and do not have name recognition. One can identify with a bookplate and an acquisition, a building, a building component, an interesting processing project, and occasionally even a named curatorship, but equipment and services such as automation enhancements are almost impossible for an individual donor or a foundation program officer to become enthusiastic about and support with a gift. This is a reality, and unless one accepts it as the obligation of the development office to indicate what the likely best match is between prospective grantor and grantee, the libraries may needlessly feel overlooked and discouraged. If a part of the library's dreams cannot be met by fund-raising because the goals are not suitable as gift or grant targets, the dream should be dropped from the list, acknowledged as dropped, and funded some other way. I fear that we are not always the best stewards of our time. The opportunity cost of pursuing a dim possibility is very high.

Libraries must be willing to alter their development priorities as circumstances change, either from an unexpected problem or an unexpected opportunity. In the case of the Stanford University Libraries, a problem arose when a fund-raising goal had to increase by $84,000 because the fire marshal and the University office responsible for assuring access for the physically limited would not approve a renovation project unless we built an additional emergency exit stair and undertook elevator modifications. Renovation projects are hard enough to fund through gifts without having to add $84,000 worth of unexpected construction costs to the goal.

In another case our development priorities were altered when we had the opportunity to acquire a significant private collection in the history of science as a bargain sale, i.e., part gift and part purchase. We are trying to underwrite a large part of the purchase price through gifts. This is one of the more difficult sorts of fund-raising since the collection has already arrived at Stanford and it has the collectors' names on it. It requires an extraordinarily selfless donor to make a gift after-the-fact for Stanford to acquire a collection with someone else's name associated with it. I cite these two examples as illustrations of how carefully determined priorities are occasionally altered by circumstances. The library development officer has to be willing to live with the disappointments of, and maintain collegial relationships with, library staff whose projects have been placed lower on the attention list as a result of newly pressing priorities. The backing of the library director is an important morale factor.

Grantors

The third noun is grantors because, obvious as it may seem, behind every gift and grant is someone or some organization who made the gift or grant. I believe that the donors, or grantors, are as important as the gifts. It is a truism in development that one receives additional gifts from donors who are thanked genuinely, promptly, and appropriately; from donors who are informed occasionally that their gift has had real meaning — for example, a selective list of titles purchased from endowed fund income; and one receives additional gifts from donors whose relationship with people, either in the library with staff or outside it with volunteers, is mutually pleasurable and satisfying. We have an obligation to donors not only to assure them over the years that an endowed fund is being managed well by the university but also that the purposes of the gift are being carried out and continue to have meaning. Another obligation is to report to donors or their families when things are not as they understood them to be, for instance when there is a change of purpose for a room named long ago for a family member now deceased.

In the case of most foundation grants and all government grants, the recipient institution is obligated to report on the use of the funds on a predetermined timetable. The library accounting office works with the principal investigator or librarian in charge of the work to prepare periodic and final financial reports and statements of progress. So there is an ongoing relationship with the grantor.

In the case of gifts from individuals, who are also grantors in this sense, the recipient institution is not usually obligated by the terms of the gift to provide periodic reports, but it is certainly wise to do so. Besides seeing that donors receive reports on the use of their funds, a donor relations program should ensure that donors of large collections or monetary gifts are honored at special luncheons or dinners with judicious use of the president's presence; included on invitation lists to library events such as major exhibition openings, dedications, and other university events as appropriate; informed when a major personnel change takes place, such as a new library director or university president; and sent a copy of the library annual report and of any specialized publications such as exhibition catalogs or program keepsakes that might be of interest.

Judgment is of course required in some of these cases. For example, at Stanford all library donors of over $200 and those who made gifts of materials appraised at over $200 receive the annual report for that year; certain donors from previous years also receive the report, many with covering letters from the library director or another library staff member as appropriate. But only about two dozen donors received a (complimentary) copy of the 96-page exhibition catalog prepared for an exhibition of books representing five centuries of botanical illustration with an emphasis on orchids. The exhibition was drawn partially from the Stanford collections but primarily from the collection, on loan, of a Stanford alumnus. The collector made a gift of seed money for an exhibition catalog publication fund that will enable the library to produce attractive catalogs for sale and thereby replenish the fund for the next catalog.

The orchid catalog included 42 beautiful illustrations, 15 of them in color. It was a gift from the library that brought some delight to the donors to whom it was sent — donors of large book funds, buildings, or collections; volunteers who had led development or other helpful committees; and prospective donors with whom we had begun gift discussions and who were deemed likely to enjoy the catalog. In all cases the orchid catalog was accompanied by a personal note, usually from the library director. In a few instances the note was from the collection development director, the head of Special Collections, or the library development officer, depending on who had the closest personal relationship with the person to whom the catalog was sent.

I want to underscore the importance of the personal relationship with the donor/grantor and those who are instrumental in others' gifts. It is widely acknowledged in development that the people who are able to make large gifts are more likely to make them when they have not only met but developed confidence in, and often also a liking for, the people who carry out the institution's work or administer it. It is extremely important for the staff to be sensitive to the financial and personal subtleties of gifts of great value, whether they are gifts of funds or gifts of collections. There is a person behind every gift or grant, and the staff must attempt to be attentive, sensitive, and mature in interpersonal relationships. I believe that a staff who learns to listen carefully to the unstated as well as the stated, and who becomes acquainted with prospective donors and grantors as people, will be less likely to fail to follow through with reports, invitations, and periodic letters of appreciation to the people who have made the gifts and grants. One must not forget to express appreciation to the volunteers who influenced gift decisions as well as to the donors.

I believe that a combination of goal orientation, hard work, and sensitivity will enable university libraries to garner their share of gifts and grants and to do this garnering continuously, not episodically. Development must be patient, sustained, and often subtle. Our biggest mistake, I have heard some say, is to be in too much of a hurry. Proposal volume is less important than proposal quality, and appropriate timing is crucial. I believe that with some of these guidelines, and with some luck, what will soar high are not only your dreams but also your gift totals.

Notes

1. Silk collage by Verina Warren, 1982.

2. Breivik, Patricia Senn and E. Burr Gibson, ed. *Funding Alternatives for Libraries*. Chicago: American Library Association, 1979. ("Outgrowth of a workshop on fundraising for libraries that was held at the Pratt Institute Graduate School of Library and Information Science in January 1976.")

3. ------------------ . Andrew J. Eaton, 129--41. First appeared in *College & Research Libraries* September 1971, 351--61.

4. Allerton Park Institute, 25th, 1979. *Organizing the Library's Support: Donors, Volunteers, Friends*. Ed. D.W. Krummel. Urbana-Champaign, Illinois: University of Illinois Graduate School of Library Science. Paper on "Friends Groups and Academic Libraries," Paul H. Mosher, 69--75.

5. Boss, Richard W. *Grant Money and How to Get It; A Handbook for Librarians*. New York: R.R. Bowker, 1980.

THE TRUTH ABOUT TRUSTS:
ONE LIBRARY'S EXPERIENCE

Pat Woodrum

Following hurricane "Alicia," rescue workers tediously made their way into an area that had been almost totally devastated by the storm. They worked for hours to remove the debris that had virtually buried a mobile home. Finally, they were able to reach the front door and, knocking loudly, called out, "this is the Red Cross." All was quiet for a moment and then a voice from within replied, "We've had some problems lately and I don't think we'll be able to contribute much this year."

Many charitable organizations are viewed in the same way as were those rescue workers; providing needed services but always seeking financial aid. Fortunately, libraries do not have that same image which makes it much easier, in some ways, to raise money.

Almost every library has financial problems to contend with at one time or another. Some of the more serious problems may be counteracted if alternate funding programs are adopted before a crisis occurs: alternate funding programs such as the establishment of a trust. The creation of a trust is relatively simple, but the development, care and feeding is time consuming and requires intricate planning and perpetual care.

This paper will describe how one library, the Tulsa City-County Library, created and developed such a trust and the lessons learned from this endeavor. In 1972, the Tulsa Library Trust was created to receive and administer contributions to and for the benefit of the library and for the advancement of literature and library science. The legal documents were prepared, free of charge, by an attorney who was a member of the Library Commission. The Trust was set up as a public foundation under Section 501 (C) (3) of the Internal Revenue Code. All contributions to the trust are tax deductible. A board was created consisting of two members appointed by the Library Commission, two members selected by the Friends and a fifth member mutually agreed upon by both groups. Two years later only $250 existed in the Trust. The untimely death of Allie Beth Martin, my predecessor, brought in numerous contributions from across the country totalling $9,000 which were set aside as a scholarship fund within the Trust. In the next few years, other memorial contributions and unsolicited donations were received; by the end of 1980 a little over $13,000 had accumulated.

About the same time, we began to witness severe financial problems being encountered by urban libraries across the country. Although our operating funds, which are derived from ad valorem taxes, were adequate to meet our current needs, no one knew what the future held for us. It was then that we began to look for alternate funding sources and decided that the Trust, already in existence, was the most advantageous vehicle to develop. A trust would enable us to strive toward excellence in services and collection development and would provide an insurance policy for the future.

I enlisted the assistance of the library's public relations officer, and together we began to plan an approach to build the Trust. Although both of us had experience in millage campaigns, neither had ever been involved in fund-raising of the magnitude of which we were about to become involved. Our first step, as librarians are often prone to do, was to conduct a literature search on the subject of trusts, followed by letters of inquiry to a number of public libraries. We learned that a few libraries had trusts for accumulating building funds, but none that we could identify had a general trust fund of the type we had decided to develop. We would, therefore, be sailing forth into virgin waters. There would be no "tried and true" pattern to follow and we simply would have to learn by first hand experience.

A survey of the immediate community appeared to be the next logical move, and we called on approximately ten business and civic leaders. The visits consisted of telling each individual of our plans to build the Trust and asking for their suggestions. The response in each case was that it was a good idea but might be hard to sell because the library was a tax-supported institution. Taking all the advice into consideration, we proceeded to the next step which was to enlist the aid of a Library Commission member who later became the Chairperson of the Commission and President of the Tulsa Library Trust. She was knowledgeable about the library, persuasive and well-known and respected throughout the community but, like the other two of us on the team, inexperienced in raising large sums of money. By now it was evident that building a trust was going to require a significant amount of time and that it would be necessary to identify a staff member who would oversee these efforts. The Public Relations officer was designated as part-time Trust Development officer, and we announced that our fund drive was officially underway.

Based on the information we had gathered thus far, we decided to form a Trust Development Committee consisting of long standing community leaders who were experienced in fund-raising. The seven member group consisted of oil men, bankers and a former mayor and was chaired by the Library Commissioner. Their expertise was primarily in the area of corporate giving, and that would be the first group we would approach. A list of potential contributors was prepared from numerous sources and was reviewed by the Committee. Using information developed on each corporation such as total assets, number of employees, past community contributions and advice of Committee members, we determined the amount to solicit from each corporation. This information helped us set a goal of two million dollars. As I look back, perhaps it was a little bold to set so high a goal for three novice fund-raisers. At one point we considered turning the project over to professional fund-raisers, and we talked with personnel from several firms. However, the Committee agreed that a sincere, low-key approach would be much more effective in our situation than a high pressure campaign conducted by individuals from outside the community.

The existence of the Library's trust was still relatively unknown to the general public; consequently, it was necessary to devise a publicity and marketing plan. Two approaches were used simultaneously; one was a series of VIP breakfasts and the other a year-long celebration of the 20th anniversary of the Library System.

The three-member development team, composed of the Library Commissioner, the Trust Development officer and myself, prepared lists of chief executive officers or key contact people in the major corporations and placed them into small groups of five to seven. A personal telephone call from the Library Commissioner invited them to attend a VIP breakfast at the Central Library with a promise that only an hour and a half would be taken from their busy schedules. Personal information pertaining to alma maters, hobbies, families, etc. on each individual was gathered from library resources, secretaries and spouses. On the appointed date, guests were served a light breakfast, shown a brief slide show and escorted on a personal tour of the main library. Department heads in each area highlighted the resources and services using the personal data gathered previously on each individual to personalize the demonstration. At the conclusion of the session, the participants were told about the Trust and informed that the three-member team would call on them within a short period of time to ask for a contribution. Immediately following the VIP tour, a letter was sent to each guest thanking him for attending the orientation and stating that we were looking forward to visiting with him in the next few weeks. Approximately two weeks later, the Team called on the potential contributor and asked for a specific amount which could be pledged over a five-year period.

The results were incredible and probably no one was more

surprised by the success of these visits than were the three of us. At first we were a little nervous about entering the hallowed offices of internationally recognized corporate giants and asking for contributions, but we were dedicated to the cause and sincerely believed in what we were doing. In every case, we were warmly received and treated in a most cordial manner. I will have to admit, however, that it was extremely difficult to remain calm and poised when we received our first $100,000 pledge, but we maintained our composure until we were on our way out of the building and privately sequestered in an elevator!

One of the pledges received was from Southwestern Bell. During the recent telephone strike, the calls from the public to the library requesting directory information increased considerably. A small article appeared in the paper applauding the library for providing this assistance during the temporary curtailment of service. I received a call from the president of Southwestern Bell the next morning saying thanks for the help and that he had a check for us. He went on to say that he little suspected the library would be coming to their aid so soon and in such a direct way after the pledge was made.

Within a 12-month period we had raised 1.1 million dollars in pledges. But the monetary rewards were only part of what was gained during that time period. We also developed a good working relationship with leaders of the corporate community, some of whom admitted that they had never been inside any of the Tulsa public libraries prior to the VIP breakfasts. Many began to send their employees to the library, and the level of activity increased so rapidly in the Business & Technology Department that it was necessary to add another staff member.

In addition to the VIP tours, and during the same time period, a massive community celebration commemorated the library system's twentieth anniversary. In addition to the system's twentieth anniversary, it was also an opportunity to recognize the Trust's tenth anniversary and to draw attention to its existence as well as seek contributions from the community at large. During a seven-month period, using every possible means, the library's past was examined, the present studied, and the future explored.

The corporate world demonstrated its confidence in the library and its desire to see us strive toward greater horizons. Another objective was to involve the total community. The theme developed for the all-encompassing celebration was, "Happy Birthday Library and Many Happy Returns."

In pursuit of this theme, Library staff and hundreds of community volunteers:

---- Prepared a multi-media slide show depicting the Library's history and presented it to community groups;

---- Ran a six-week mystery contest on a local radio station with clues that could only be found in a library; the winner received a $1,000 check from the broadcasting company;

---- Presented public service spots on radio and television stations;

--- Hosted a birthday party at each of the 21 library facilities;

--- Featured 21 Oklahoma authors in programs at each library;

--- Designed and conducted a children's summer reading program based on the birthday theme;

--- Sponsored a three-day storytelling festival;

--- Conducted oral history interviews with people who were instrumental in the library's development;

---- Found a benefactor and commissioned an artist to produce a multi-media collage depicting the library's history;

---- Worked with a local television station to produce a prime time thirty minute special on the library;

---- Received a contribution to write and publish an 80-page history of the library;

--- Established a Library Hall of Fame and inducted the initial members;

---- Presented a series of six programs featuring internationally known authors;

---- Offered numerous programs to highlight special collections of the Library; and

---- Sponsored a community-wide formal dinner and program in the Central Library with a well-known speaker as a finale to the celebration and to recognize the major Trust contributors.

The celebration accomplished many things. As one can well imagine, an intensive, seven-month project took its toll on the staff members most closely involved. By the end of the project, everyone was very weary, to say the least. But the positive results were:

1) The public was more aware of the Library and what it had to offer,

2) The individuals and groups who had played significant roles in the establishment and development of the library were identified and recognized for posterity,

3) At the end of the fiscal year, circulation statistics showed a record increase of 15 percent, and

4) The Trust was identified as the entity to receive contributions for the benefit of the Library.

In retrospect, the celebration was well worth all the effort that went into it. Less than one year after the completion of the celebration, the endowment had received approximately $700,000 in cash contributions. The fund is managed by the Trust Department of a local bank and last year earned $56,000 in interest.

The Trust Board decided at the outset that only the interest earned will be spent and that the principal will be left untouched. In addition to the corporate contributions, monetary gifts varying in size from $10 to $50,000 were received from individuals. In one case, an elderly gentleman who patronizes the library almost everyday heard about the Trust and contributed $11,000 worth of stock. On another occasion, visitors from the Netherlands and friends of the Library Commissioner toured the Central Library. They responded with a surprise donation of $10,000 and a pledge of $40,000 more. Proposals have recently been submitted to several foundations for challenge grants as we continue forward in our drive to raise two million dollars.

If I were to summarize my experience in fund-raising over the last two years and offer specific advice to others interested in embarking upon a similar venture, I would suggest the following approach:

1) Determine the Need
> Be able to state the need in clear and concise terms. Libraries, in particular public libraries, are very easy to market because they are designed for all age groups and for all segments of a community.

2) Survey the Climate

Analyze the community's philanthropic base and research the current economic trends. Review the status of other community fund-raising campaigns.

3) Seek Support of Community Leaders

Meet with the leaders in the community and ask for their advice as well as their support. People tend to be protective and supportive of a project if they have been consulted in the formative stages.

4) Select a Chairperson

A good chairperson is an essential element in any campaign. The qualifications of a good chairperson are that he or she must be genuinely concerned about the cause, willing to dedicate many hours of hard work and be well-known and respected in the community.

5) Designate Staff Liaison

An energetic, creative and knowledgeable staff member is also a key factor in a successful campaign.

6) Appoint an Advisory Group

Seek out individuals who have some name recognition and credibility in the community and who have been involved in other fund-raising activities. It is also helpful to select persons who are known for their personal or corporate philanthropic activities.

7) Set a Goal

A goal should be realistic but also challenging. One method in determining a goal is to list potential contributors and the amount that will be requested from each. A total of this amount should serve as a good barometer in arriving at a goal.

8) Design a Plan of Action

There are many approaches to fund-raising, but selecting the appropriate one for your community is one of the most important decisions that has to be made.

9) Analyze the Target Group

Learn everything possible about the potential contributors. In the case of corporations, determine the number of employees, type of business holdings, size of assets, organizations contributed to in the past and, if possible, average size of contributions.

10) Implement the Campaign
The early days of the actual campaign are often the most difficult. After you are successful a couple of times, your confidence level will build steadily.

11) Devise Methods of Recognition
Even though some contributors may ask to remain anonymous, all efforts should be recognized in one way or another. A plaque, certificate, small gift, or even just a letter is appropriate to express appreciation for their contribution and interest in the library.

12) Maintain Contact with Contributors
Develop ways to stay in contact with contributors after the campaign, such as sending annual reports and letters describing accomplishments resulting from their contributions. They became a library supporter when they made their contribution; do not lose their interest by neglecting them.

In closing, I would like to read a quotation which reflects my feelings toward fund-raising for libraries. It was written by Thomas Broce who was for many years an outstanding fund-raiser for the University of Oklahoma:

The excitement that comes with raising money does not lie in impressive gift-record charts. It lies instead in that glow one feels when the person with the skills to make things happen comes in contact with a person with the resources to make an investment that will pay significant benefits to many generations. When the two come together, they move mountains![1]

Note

1. Broce, Thomas. *Fund Raising: The Guide to Raising Money from Private Sources*. Norman, University of Oklahoma Press, 1979. p3.

Bibliography

Broce, Thomas. *Fund Raising: The Guide to Raising Money from Private Sources*. Norman, University of Oklahoma Press, 1979.

Flanagan, Joan. *The Grass Roots Fund Raising Book: How to Raise Money in ,Your Community*. Chicago, The Swallow Press, 1977.

Hillman, Howard. *The Art of Winning Corporate Grants*. New York, The Vanguard Press, Inc., 1980.

Sharpe, Robert F. *The Planned Giving Idea Book: Creative Ways to Increase the Income of Your Institution*. Nashville, Thomas Nelson, Inc., 1978.

Warner, Irving R. *The Art of Fund Raising*. New York, Harper and Row, 1975.

INTEGRATING FUND-RAISING INTO THE ADMINISTRATION OF UNIVERSITY LIBRARIES: GOALS, PLANS, STRATEGIES

Robin N. Downes

This paper describes library development programs which have, for the most part, been effective in a medium-sized university library in a large Southwestern city. Excluded from the paper are issues and methods dealing with government grants and sponsored research. The discussion concentrates on the acquisition of gifts from individuals, corporations, and foundations. The emphasis is on large gifts. Included in the discussion are goals which will be controversial in many universities. Not considered open to question, however, is the underlying philosophy that fund-raising should be a basic administrative responsibility of a university library, that no one else in a university can provide the direction and insight underlying a successful program, and that professional satisfaction and personal pleasure, mixed with healthy doses of frustration, await the successful practitioner of the art.

It is the argument of this paper that fund-raising for university libraries must be given equal priority with that for the colleges, that friends of the library organizations must become re-oriented more directly to fund-raising, that departments of special collections must undergo a drastic change from traditional roles to provide a focus for fund-raising and to support directly instructional and research programs, that every major gift to a university which supports expansion or upgrading of an academic program should have a percentage allocated to the library, that every major college or university-wide fund-raising effort should have a library component, and that university library administration and patterns of organization must be changed to make these results possible. It is a corollary of these arguments that responsibility for making the library co-equal with the colleges, for assuring active participation by the library in fund-raising at the college and university levels, and of course for changing patterns of library administration and organization, rests with the libraries. Because some of these arguments are controversial and deal with zones of interest, they obviously are long-term goals as well as, in some cases, achievable short-term plans.

The first and overriding conclusion to be drawn from this menu of responsibilities is that a substantial investment of library or university staff resources must be made to achieve the desired results. It is the viewpoint of this paper that the amount of effort and the specialized skills required mandate the creation of a position of library development officer. Some of the duties of such a position have traditionally been carried out by a library's chief administrator. Other pieces of the assignment have typically been performed by a head of a special collections department. In a few cases, university development officers have become interested in library development programs, usually on the initiative of the chief administrator of the library. Such traditional methods have at times been spectactularly successful. But the typical university library cannot depend on acquiring general administrative officers with the unique mix of talents and personalities which has made such success stories possible.

If a library development officer position is created, a decision must be reached on locating it in the library administration or within the university development office. The University of Houston Libraries have benefited greatly from having the position located in the library administration. But as is characteristic of development programs, local conditions may make a different arrangement desirable. The strongest argument for placing the position in the library administration is the newness of the idea that fund-raising is a principal responsibility of the library. It can also be argued that an academic unit so different from the colleges requires special approaches to fund-raising, and that only within the library can the necessary understanding be developed. Based on the experience of the University of Houston Libraries, the ideal solution would be a position budgeted in the library, and with an adjunct position in the university development office. The adjunct role would provide assurance that the library's participation in college and university-wide fund-raising programs is not forgotten. It would also assist with the coordination of library fund-raising programs and those of the colleges and departments of the university.

One of the most satisfying conditions of fund-raising at the University of Houston Libraries was the result of the appointment of just such a library development officer. This position was created by the Libraries not for any of the logical reasons set forth in this paper, but because fund-raising at the university level was in a state of transition at the time of the appointment. At that time, it seemed definite that two years or more would pass before direction and support at the university-wide level would be in place. And even when that leadership was in place, on what precedent could assurance be based that the library would be treated as a co-equal with the colleges in setting fund-raising priorities. In fund-raising, as in life, the Lord helps those best who help themselves.

The range of responsibility of the library development officer is exceptionally broad. Among the most urgent is the mission of assisting in making the library a visible presence in the social and cultural life of the university and beyond. This is a task which one person, working alone, has small hope of achieving. In cooperation with librarians and faculty, and with the help of university offices of media relations and publications, it is possible for a library development officer to achieve a great deal.

The task of making the library a visible presence is constant and demanding. But it must be done, and sustained, if a university library is to be perceived as co-equal with the colleges in its needs for a share in external fund-raising. Its mission must of course be argued persuasively and often by its principal administrators. But the audience to be reached is far broader, and presenting the case to this larger community takes many forms. Reaching these groups means issuing a newsletter addressed to the interest of the faculty and campus administration and a second newsletter addressed to external friends and supporters, and not just to the official friends of the libraries organization. It means knowing the editors and feature writers of the major newspapers in the community. It means knowing key contact persons at the community educational television station and commercial television stations. All this, again, is supplementary to the normal contacts between the library administration and the faculty senate, other academic councils, and the university administration. But it is a vital supplement if library values and needs are to achieve visibility and if this visibility is to be followed by understanding and support from within and outside the university.

Making the libraries "visible" to the campus and the community is only marginally useful unless the message transmitted reflects the thrust of strategic planning by the libraries and the university. Strategic planning is based on a vision of the mission and goals of the institution. Realizing this, it is obvious why fund-raising officers report directly to the highest levels of administration. Library development officers naturally, then, should report to the director of libraries. Whether a development officer for libraries is best located in the library administrative structure or in the university-wide development office is a separate question. The case can be argued both ways, as shown previously in this paper.

A second major responsibility of the library development officer is the identification of potential sources of private gifts and grants from foundations and government agencies. This assignment requires a set of personal and professional contacts as extensive as the "public relations" tasks just outlined. It may also require extensive travel to consult personally with officers of foundations and federal agencies.

41

Writing skills are indispensable for the drafting of proposal letters and full proposals.

In describing a third area of responsibility of the library development officer, mention must first be made of the desirability of closer integration of special collections departments with the collection policies and service programs of university libraries. Should, for example, a special collections department be re-configured into a limited number of clearly-defined program areas? With few exceptions, staff resources and book funds for special collections could then be concentrated exclusively on these programs. As an example of such program concentration, a new program called the Creative Writing/Performing Arts Archives has been established in the University of Houston Libraries. The Archives build on an already important collection of the manuscripts, correspondence and memorabilia of well-known national and regional novelists, poets, and dramatists. The Archives provide a direct link with a strong Creative Writing Program offered by the University of Houston. The Creative Writing Program offers degrees through the doctorate, and the resources of the Archives have the potential to support the Creative Writing Program and at the same time to benefit from contacts with the prominent writers who teach in the Program.

Public relations activities centered around such areas of concentration selected thus far as programs for Special Collections have resulted in major news articles and editorials in the major Houston newspapers, feature articles in alumni magazines, television news and feature programs on educational and commercial television stations, and feature articles in Sunday newspaper magazine sections. The President of the University and major donors to Special Collections are prominent players in these media presentations. Other activities include benefit performances by local theatre companies and receptions at the home of the President of the University for faculty, librarians, friends of the libraries, and major donors. As an example of one such benefit event, a dinner at the home of the University President resulted in contributions of over $50,000 to the Creative Writing/Performing Arts Archives.

The point cannot be made too often that such fund-raising programs are successful only if the library is highly visible and only if countless contacts throughout the university and the community are first made and then maintained. They are made by individual contacts. They are sustained not only by these same contacts, but by frequent library-centered events, maximum publicity in all local media, and by library publications which meet high standards of editorial and production quality, and which are targeted on appropriate interest groups.

Closely related to the organization and purpose of a special collections department is the friends of the library association. In the traditional mode, a friends group represents persons who are interested in books and libraries, and who join together to express this interest and support in library programs. Some friends associations are concerned with the strengths of the collections generally. But in most cases, a particular cause for pride lies in the various collections that constitute special collections. Many of these collections result from the gifts-in-kind of members of the friends associations. A friends association may also support the library's building program and physical improvements of existing facilities.

Through these contributions, the friends ideally would enable the library to make additions to the collections or improvements in physical facilities which otherwise would be beyond the resources of the library's annual budget. A friends association may also support series of lectures on scholarly matters and thus enhance the life of the university community. Above all, the Friends, ideally, understand and enjoy the world of books and libraries, and the meeting point which they represent between the world and the life of the mind.

It is argued here that a more formal fund-raising structure should be added to the traditional friends association. In the University of Houston a proposal is being discussed which called for the Friends to sponsor and jointly participate in a Foundation Fund in which the membership of the Friends joins hands with a Foundation Fund Board of Trustees and the University of Houston Foundation in fund-raising campaigns to benefit the Libraries. The Foundation Fund would be intended to serve as a "fiduciary" extension of the Friends. It would act in the interest of and in coordination with the Friends. Three-fifths of the Board of the Foundation Fund would, hypothetically, be composed of members of the Friends, the Chairman of the Friends would be a member, and the Coordinator of the Friends — who also serves as the Library Development Officer — would be Secretary of the Board. The Foundation Fund therefore in a real sense would act on the behalf of the Friends.

The Foundation would then serve as a point of contact with potential contributors to fund-raising efforts of the Libraries. The creation of a Foundation Fund as an arm of the Friends would be a recognition of the multiple facets of the Friends. One of these facets is the raising of funds to provide the Libraries over the years with those elements of quality and distinction which only stem from the involvement of outstanding individuals in the destiny of an institution.

The Foundation Fund already has an important task to deal with which has profound impact on the quality of the Libraries and the University. This effort involves direction and leadership of a campaign to raise $1,000,000 over the next three years to match a special grant from the University System of $2,000,000 from endowment funds.

Systematic planning for fund-raising is comparable in one sense to teaching a butterfly to fly in a straight line. As we present our arguments to individuals, to foundations and to corporations, we are reminded again and again of what a prominent writer referred to as "the fragility and luck of life." Even so, administrators should think of fund-raising programs in the terms they would use for any program where improvement is needed. These terms include goals, plans, strategies, methodologies, organization, and — always most important — talent in key positions. Because fund-raising is not yet established as a principal program of university library administration, and because of the elusive nature of development work, the setting of goals is the most difficult of these terms. Any attempt to set standards for results to be achieved will inevitably be arbitrary. Recognizing its arbitrary character, however, it is the argument of this paper that university libraries should expect that a percentage of gifts for support of academic programs equal to the library's share of the educational and general fund budget should go to support library programs. And the minimum goal of the library itself should be ten percent of the library's annual book budget.

A number of strong positions have been taken in this paper. The dominant theme is that fund-raising must be a principal charge to the university library administration. Second, the library must be treated as a co-equal with the colleges when university-wide fund-raising campaigns are conducted. Third, when such university-wide campaigns result in expanded academic programs, a percentage of the gifts should be allocated to library support. Fourth, to pay their dues, libraries must be equipped to contribute as equals with the colleges to the arduous, frustrating, and complex tasks of publicizing to the support community their role and value in the educational process. Fifth, the professional skills required to build and sustain such a program should be sought in a library development officer, budgeted in the library and with adjunct reporting status in the university development office. Sixth, the organization of a special collections department should be re-examined as to its contribution to education programs and its relationship to fund-raising. Seventh, the organization of the traditional friends association should be changed to more directly relate its efforts to fund-raising.

Opportunities exist for supplementing library funds through these methods, often with crucial impact on the quality of the library's programs. Administrators should not expect to achieve long-term success, however, unless the development program is directed, staffed, funded, and supported as would any other vital on-going program of the library. The building of a successful program may require years of sustained effort by persons with a high level of professional skills. Spurts of occasional. success, dependent on individual talents of key administrators of the library, are invaluable to the university. But lasting success must be built on a solid program which is a permanent part of the administration of a university library.

FUND-RAISING FOR LIBRARIES

Albert Milano

Outside fund-raising consultants are another option for development work. Whether to have professional fund-raisers actually solicit gifts or only to organize and supervise a program is essentially a local decision. In any event, many successful development efforts are transferable. The ideas which work in one program may well be the basis for a good development effort at another library.

The following material was prepared by Albert Milano, General Manager of the Dallas Theater Center and President of The Milano Group, fund-raising consultants. Mr. Milano has been quite successful as a fund-raiser for the Dallar Theater Center as well as a consultant for many other enterprises. The following outline and accompanying documents provide useful insight into organizing a development drive and offer useful advice on the many details of a fund-raising program.

FUND-RAISING FOR LIBRARIES

OUTLINE

I. **EXAMINE SOURCES OF INCOME**
   A. Endowments or investments
   B. Private source gifts or grants (individuals, foundations, corporations, volunteers)
   C. Tax-based revenue or grants
   D. Memberships — tuition — sales of goods (encourages future gifts)

II. **BUILD COMPREHENSIVE FINANCIAL PLAN**

   — Essential Start for Fundraising Efforts —

   A. Pinpoint your mission:
      the facilities
      the people   needed to carry out program
      the monies
   B. Estimate total funding needs — short and long-term income potential
   C. Establish a recommended time frame for accomplishing goal.

III. **INGREDIENTS OF FUND RAISING**
   A. Confidence in the organization
      — Donor must believe gift will be well used.
      Factors:
      1) How well do you manage the program?
      2) How do you manage your finances?
      3) How strong are your trustees?
      4) How strong is your staff?
      5) What is the distinction of your past record?
      6) What is the credibility of your plan?
   B. Urgency and importance of your case
      Questions:
      1) Is your program important or urgent?
      2) To whom?
      3) What needs does it meet?
      4) Does it present a new idea?
      5) Are you the toy of the well-to-do or the responsibility of the entire community?

C. Development of donor constituency
   Examine past donors (people, companies, foundations).
   Find others like them who have not been asked.

IV. ACTION
   A. The gift table
   B. Volunteer leadership
      1) A handful of leaders raise 75% of the money.
      2) 10% of donors will give 85% of the total.
      3) Leaders must be Board members.
   C. Board gives first!
      1) Board recruits and solicits other solicitors.
      2) Development Council if Board is weak and case is strong.
   D. Biggest non-Board gifts next.
      1) Individuals
         a) Making the big job bite sized
            i) One of $5,000 raised by the Board members who gave $5,000
            ii) One of $2,500 raised by one or both Board members who gave $5,000
            iii) Ten of $1,000 raised by three or more Board members who gave $1,000
         b) People give to Peers
            i) Staff does not solicit.
            ii) All calls in person.
      2) Corporations
         – Divisional Set-Up with Flexibility
         a) Recruit leader who gives a lot
         b) Recruit division leaders who are pacesetters
            – Leading Corporation – Leading Gift –
         c) Get leaders to solicit their own:
            i) Law Firms
            ii) Ad and Public Relations Agencies
            iii) Accountants
      3) Foundations
         a) Family vs. professional (peer/staff)
         b) Uniqueness; model building
         c) Letter of inquiry
         d) Proposal

V. MATERIALS
   A. The proposal or case statement
   B. Records
   C. Prospect cards and assignment sheets
   D. Sample letters

A FUND-RASING KIT

The following kit is an example of useful documents and forms for organizing a development project. Although the examples are for a theatre, they should be useful for other types of nonprofit institutions.

THE MILANO GROUP

STANDARD FUND RAISING GIFT TABLE
$100,000 Goal

Gifts	Amount	Totals
One	$15,000	$15,000
Two	7,500	15,000
Three	5,000	15,000
Four	2,500	10,000
(Ten Gifts . . . . .equal $55,000)		
Twenty	1,000	20,000
Fifty	below 1,000	25,000
(Eighty gifts . . . . .equal $100,000)		

Board of Trustee Segment

One	$15,000	$15,000
One	7,500	7,500
One	5,000	5,000
Two	2,500	5,000
Five	1,000	5,000
(Ten gifts. . . . . .equal $37,500)		

Gifts	Amount	Totals
	Gifts from Individuals	
One	$5,000	$5,000
One	2,500	2,500
Ten	1,000	10,000
Twenty-five	below $1,000	$12,500
(Thirty-seven gifts . . . . equal $30,000)		

	Gifts from Corporations	
One	$7,500	$7,500
One	5,000	5,000
One	2,500	2,500
Five	1,000	5,000
Twenty-five	below $1,000	15,500
(Thirty-three gifts . . . . equal $32,500)		

DALLAS THEATER CENTER

3636 Turtle Creek Blvd., Dallas, Texas 75219-5598 (214)526-8210

CORPORATE DIVISION, Charles Foster, Campaign Chairman

I.   Energy Division — Guy Marcus, Chairman
                     Goal: $90,000
       A. Major oil
       B. Independent oil
       C. Oil service companies
       D. Utilities

II.   Finance Division — Gerald Czarnecki, Chairman
                     Goal: $60,000
       A. Banks, savings and loans, Clearing House
       B. Insurance and finance companies
       C. Brokers
       D. CPA's

III.   Real Estate Division — Jerold Davis, Chairman
                     Goal: $30,000
       A. Brokers
       B. Contractors
       C. Development companies
       D. Architects

IV.   Manufacturing Division — Ed Robertson, Chairman
                     Goal: $45,000
       A. Electronics firms
       B. General manufacturing

V.   Consumer Trade Division — Dennis Reaves, Chairman
                     Goal: $75,000
       A. Retail
           1. Major department stores
          2. Minor stores and shops
          3. Manufacturers and suppliers
       B. Food and beverage distributors
       C. Advertising and public relations firms
       D. Professional (doctors, lawyers, etc.)
       E. Miscellaneous

VI.   Small Business Division — Anna Gardner, Chairman

3636 Turtle Creek Blvd., Dallas, Texas 75219-5598 (214)526-8210

KEYS TO EFFECTIVE CALLS
FOR
THE DALLAS THEATER CENTER

1983 SUSTAINING FUND DRIVE

I.   *Preparation*

    A. Be thoroughly familiar with the "story" of this effort, the validity of the Theater Center's programs and what they mean to the Center and the City of Dallas.

    B. By phone or letter, ask for an appointment to discuss the program.

    C. *Make personal visits.* Experience proves that the large majority of prospects seen personally will give. Letters or telephone conversations often result in gifts much less than the prospect's potential.

    D. Have in mind an appropriate amount or range of gift for the prospect to consider. It is important for you to think in terms of the *most* a prospect could give if he or she really wanted to.

II.   *Tell the Story of Dallas Theater Center's Needs,*
    But Be a Good Listener, Too

    A. Go through the rationale for the Sustaining Fund with your prospect, referencing key points of the presentation which might appeal to that person. Ask for reactions as you proceed.

    B. Stress the record of service of the Center, the merit and benefits of the objectives — not simply the "campaign" or fund raising goal.

    C. Use a positive, enthusiastic approach based on sincerity.

D. Encourage the prospect to ask questions about the Theater Center and its plans. If you cannot answer a question, ask for an opportunity to return with a complete answer. The development office will give you the needed information.

F. Use examples of other gifts.

III. *Ask for a Gift*

A. Set your sights high. Ask for generous support. In so doing, you pay the prospect and the campaign a compliment.

B. At the very least, suggest a giving level or range, "We would like you to consider a gift of $----------- or "in the range of $----------- to $----------- ."

C. Remind them that all gifts are tax deductible.

D. Don't press them for a decision on the first visit. Ask the prospect to think about it, and offer to see him again in a week to ten days.

E. If the prospect needs more time for a decision, leave the Theater Center Proposal and contribution form.

F. If the prospect declines making a gift, make every effort to leave him with a positive impression of the Theater Center, its future and the campaign.

IV. Inform the development office of the results of your work.

V. Relax and enjoy being an ambassador for an institution which deserves great success.

DALLAS THEATER CENTER

A Proposal To

3636 Turtle Creek Blvd.
214/526-8210

DALLAS THEATER CENTER

The Facts

The Dallas Theater Center . . .

- is more than four times larger than the next largest theater in Dallas.

- has more subscribers than any other arts institution in Dallas, including the Dallas Symphony's classical concerts.

- has a larger budget than the Dallas Opera.

- is the only theater in Dallas which has a community outreach program for all the citizens of Dallas.

- has one of the strongest educational programs for children of any theater in the country . . . 400 young people are enrolled this year.

- will reach more than 150,000 Dallas citizens this year through its various programs.

- earns a full 61% of its income from *ticket sales* . . . the highest of all the performing arts in Dallas.

Recent Initiatives

The Dallas Theater Center is actively working to raise the artistic level of its productions to the highest national standards.

How?

- By hiring eminent director Michael Langham, currently head of the drama program at Juilliard School and associate director of the Stratford Festival, to serve as artistic advisor to the theater for the next year.

- By selecting a permanent artistic director, under Mr. Langham's guidance, before the start of the 1983-84 season.

- By moving toward a higher level of stage productions within the next two years. That commitment is being defined in the current season with the extensive use of experienced Equity actors. DTC's February 1983 production of *A Lesson from Aloes* (starring Oscar and Emmy award nominee Paul Winfield) exemplifies the thrust toward exceptional quality of performance.

- By increasing its commitment to present the highest quality touring productions in Dallas, such as *Amadeus* which is scheduled for this spring at the Majestic.

- By significantly expanding its programs for young persons. This will mean more performances of plays for children, as well as expanding the Teen-Children's Theater program to reach more students through branch locations.

The Cost of our Season

Dallas Theater Center will earn $3,368,000 in 1982-83.

61% from earned income
(ticket sales, tours, tuition, special events)

13% from public grants and donated services

26% from fund raising

Dallas Theater Center will spend $3,368,000 in 1982-83.

67% for production and payroll

23% for conservatory, faculty, and administrative costs

10% for marketing and development

Dallas Theater Center must raise $1,043,000 by August 31, 1983, to meet its fund-raising goal for the 1982-83 fiscal year.

DALLAS THEATER CENTER

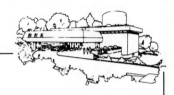

Contribution Form

MAIL TO:

Sustaining Fund
Dallas Theater Center
3636 Turtle Creek Blvd.
Dallas, Texas 75219

FILL IN AMOUNT:

We are happy to pledge $_____
to help sustain the programs and
services of the Dallas Theater Center

CHOOSE ONE:

A) Enclosed is our contribution

B) Please bill us for our pledge

Indicate name and
business address
if appropriate:

_____
Name

_____
Title

_____
Business Address

_____
Home Address

CORPORATE OR FOUNDATION

Company _____

Mailing Address _____ City _____ Zip _____

Contact _____ Title _____

Phone Main line _____ Direct _____ Secretary _____

GIVING HISTORY

Year	Amount	Solicitor	Year	Amount	Solicitor

OTHER INFORMATION

INDIVIDUAL

Name _____ Spouse _____

Address _____ City _____ Zip _____

Business affiliation _____

Phone - Home _____ Business _____ Other _____

GIVING HISTORY

Year	Amount	Solicitor	Year	Amount	Solicitor

OTHER INFORMATION

_____

DALLAS HISTORICAL SOCIETY PROSPECT CARD

Name of Prospect _____

Home/mailing address _____

City _____ Zip _____

Business _____

Business Address _____

City _____ Zip _____

Spouse or Contact _____

Home Phone _____

Position _____

Business Phone _____

GIVING HISTORY

Year	Amount	Solicitor
____	_____	_____
____	_____	_____
____	_____	_____
____	_____	_____
____	_____	_____
____	_____	_____
____	_____	_____

GOAL $ _____

This card is for the volunteer's information only, and should be used to record any changes relative to the individuals. When the solicitation is complete, return this card with comments to the Development Office, Dallas Historical Society, P.O. Box 26038, Dallas, Texas 75226.

PHONE & CORRESPONDENCE CONTACT RECORD

Date of Contacts _____ Results _____

COMMENTS

DRAFT OF A SAMPLE FOLLOW-UP LETTER

(To be typed on solicitor's letterhead)

Date

Name
Address
Address

Dear

It was good to have an opportunity to meet with you today about the Dallas Theater Center.

On behalf of that institution, I am writing to thank you in advance for considering a contribution in the range of $-------- to $---------. Of course, your contribution would be tax deductible.

I believe that there is no organization in Dallas that better exemplifies a broad commitment not only to quality and entertainment, but also to raising the quality of life in this city. At the same time, the Theater Center is now moving toward ever greater financial stability . . . they are experiencing a dramatic increase in broad-based corporate and community philanthropic support.

I urge you to participate in this effort.

Thank you very much for considering this proposal. I will be back in touch with you after you have had a few days to think it over.

Of course, I am at your service should you have any questions in the meantime.

Cordially,

BIBLIOGRAPHY

Rodney M. Hersberger

This bibliography offers selected readings for further consideration for library development. The arrangement is by broad topics to
assist the user. Some of the entries may not deal directly with library
development. These entries do, however, address fund raising and
development issues, primarily for higher education.

GIFTS

Brown, J.J. "All About Planned Giving." *Trusts and Estates* 119
(12): 744–52. December 1978.

Crafter, D. "Memorial Gifts Often Overlooked in Fund Raising."
Fund Raising Management 13(2): 34–35. April 1982.

Davis, M. "The Untapped Resource: Corporate Matching Gifts."
Fund Raising Management 14(3): 20–24. May 1983.

"Donating or Selling Your Collection to an Institution." In Wilson,
R.A.J., *Modern Book Collecting*. Knopf, 1980. p. 211–15.

Erwin, J. "Fundraising." In *Friends of Libraries Sourcebook*. ALA,
1980. p. 68–76.

Kemp, E.C. *Manuscript Solicitation for Libraries, Special Collections,
Museums and Archives*. Libraries Unlimited, 1978. 204 p.

Leonhardt, T.W. "Gift Appraisals: A Practical Approach." *Library
Acquisitions* 3(2): 77–9. 1979.

Moerschbaecher, L.S. "Integrating Planned Giving into the Fund
Raising Program." *Trusts and Estates* 122(10): 35–38. October,
1983.

Oster, G. "Local Business May Have Money for the Asking." *American Libraries* 11:373–4. June 1980.

Plinio, A.J. "Corporate Contributions: Go Beyond Fundraising to Resource Raising." *Fund Raising Management* 13(10): 58--59. December 1982.

Prentice, A.E. "Gifts, Grants, and Bequests." In Young, V.G., ed., *Library Trustee*, 3d ed. Bowker, 1978. p. 66--71.

Schenck, W.Z. "Evaluating and Valuing Gift Materials." *Library Acquisitions* 6(1): 33–40. 1982.

Stroup, T. "Donor as Archivist." *American Archivist* 42:465--6. October 1979.

FOUNDATIONS

Berry, J.N. "Positive Force or Added Complication? The Question of the Foundation Library Committee." *Library Journal* 105: 356–8. February 1, 1980.

Buckman, T.R. "Foundation Funding." In *Funding Alternatives for Libraries*. ALA, 1979. p. 101–23.

Dunlop, D. "Library Partner in an Austere Economy: The Foundation Center." *Wilson Library Bulletin* 57: 133–8. October 1982.

Lambeth, T. "Libraries, Foundations and the 1980's." *North Carolina Libraries* 39: 19–23. Summer 1981.

Pinkney, G. "Funding for the Arts." In *Library and the Contemporary Arts*. Wayne State University, Division of Library Science, 1977. p. 87--100.

Sheldon, B. "A Proposal Primer." In *Bowker Annual of the Library and Book Trade Information*. 20th ed. Bowker, 1975.

Van Ness, C. *Winning Foundation and Corporate Grants*. Resource paper no. 17. National Council for Resource Development, 1978.

PUBLIC RELATIONS

Breivik, P.S. "Public Relations and Publicity." In *Funding Alternatives for Libraries*. ALA, 1979. p. 27–31.

Edsall, M.S. *Library Promotion Handbook*. Oryx Press; Mansell. 1980. 244 p.

Huntsinger, J.E. "Mix of Right Ingredients Produces Satisfied Donors." *Fund Raising Management* 11(3): 48–49. May 1980.

Livingston, B. "How to Tap Funding from Private/Public Sources." *Library Journal* 104: 2610–11. December 15, 1979.

Wruck, Craig C. "Development Officer's Role Emphasizes Relationships." *Fund Raising Management* 11(10): 14–15. December 1980.

FRIENDS ORGANIZATIONS

Allerton Park Institute, 1979. *Organizing the Library's Support: Donors, Volunteers, Friends*. Ed. by D.W. Krammel. Univ. of Illinois, Graduate School of Library and Information Science. 1980. 119 p.

Cole, J.Y. "Good Ideas for Friends' Groups; A Report on a Forum Sponsored by the Center for the Book and Friends of Libraries USA." *Library of Congress Information Bulletin* 40: 79–80. March 6, 1981.

Dolnick, S., comp. *Directory of Friends of Libraries Groups in the United States*. ALA. LAMA. Public Relations Section. Friends of Libraries Committee, 1978. 297 p.

Friends of Libraries Source Book. Ed. by S. Dolnick. ALA, 1980. 165 p.

Gwyn, A. "Friends of the Library." *College and Research Libraries* 36(4): 272–82. July 1975.

O'Neill, R.R. "On the Organization, Governance, and Value of Friends of the Library Organizations." *Library Occurrent* 26: 231–6+. August 1979.

Pennell, H.B., ed. *Find Out Who Your Friends Are: A Practical Manual for the Formation of Library Support Groups*. Friends of the Free Library of Philadelphia, 1978. 66 p.

Riffel, M. "Establishing a Friends Group." *Arkansas Librarian* 37: 12–14. March 1980.

Scupholm, P.T. "Portraits of Friends Organizations." In *Friends of Libraries Sourcebook*. ALA, 1980. p. 99–114.

Wallace, S.L. "Trustees and the Friends of the Library." In Young, V.G., ed., *Library Trustee*, 3d ed. Bowker, 1978. p. 130–80.

MISCELLANEOUS ARTICLES

Allen, T.W. "Strategic Management: A Tool for Improving Fund Raising in Higher Education." *Management Focus* 28(2): 675. March/April 1981.

Duca, Diane. "New Grants-Writer of the 80's Must Research, Know Market." *Fund Raising Management* 10(7): 54–55. February 1980.

Duca, Diane. "New Strategy for Writing Proposals Now Necessary." *Fund Raising Management* 12(12): 58. February 1982.

Dyer, E.R. "Consultant's Role in Library Development." *International Federation of Library Associations Journal* 7(4): 352–9. 1981.

Harman, W.J. "Strategic Plans Increase Capital Campaign Success." *Fund Raising Management* 12(6): 38–41. August 1981.

Kunec, J.L. "Market Your Mission by Stating Your Case." *Fund Raising Management* 13(3): 26–31. May 1982.

Mann, H.S. "How to Raise Funds with Real Property." *Trusts and Estates* 119(12): 58–61. December 1978.

Scanlon, W.F. "Survey Looks at Academically Trained Fund Raisers." *Fund Raising Management* 12(4): 30–34. June 1981.

Schneiter, P.H. "New Survey of College Fund Raising Challenges Old Ideas." *Fund Raising Management* 12(9): 36–39, 67. September 1981.

Soukup, D.J. "A Markov Analysis of Fund-Raising Alternatives." *Journal of Marketing Research* 20(3): 314–19. August 1983.

Stocker, L.E. "Market Research Points Out Donor Perceptions." *Fund Raising Management* 13(7): 28, 30, 32–33. September 1982.

DISSERTATIONS

Betts, F.M., III. *The Development of Objectives for a Training Program in Fund Raising for Educational Administrators.* Ed.D., University of Pennsylvania, 1977. 232 p.

Colida, L.S., Jr. *Fund Raising in Private Higher Education: An Analysis of the Role of the Development Officer as Administrator at Selected Institutions.* Ph.D., Loyola University, 1980. 342 p.

Ishoy, V.A. *Fund Raising, A Function of Development in Financing Higher Education.* Ed.D., Brigham Young University, 1972. 263 p.

McGinnis, D.R. *A Study of Fund Raising Programs at Selected State Colleges and Regional Universities.* Ed.D., University of Georgia, 1980. 186 p.

Paton, G.J. *Correlates of Successful College Fund Raising.* Ph.D., Stanford University, 1983. 191 p.

Pickett, W.L. *An Assessment of the Effectiveness of Fund Raising Policies of Private Undergraduate Colleges.* Ph.D., University of Denver, 1977. 175 p.

Sherratt, G.R. *A Study of the Methods and Techniques Used in Fund-Raising at Selected Public Universities.* Ph.D., Michigan State University, 1975. 468 p.

Stout, G.W. *A Study of Fund-Raising Programs at Selected Public Multicampus Universities.* Ed.D., The University of Tennessee, 1977. 180 p.

INDEX